Da’esh (ISIS) and Al Ghabra’a

(Play)

To watch the play, please scan the following QR Code:
Da'esh (ISIS) and Al Ghabra'a

Dr. Sultan bin Muhammad Al-Qasimi

Da'esh (ISIS) and Al Ghabra'a

(Play)

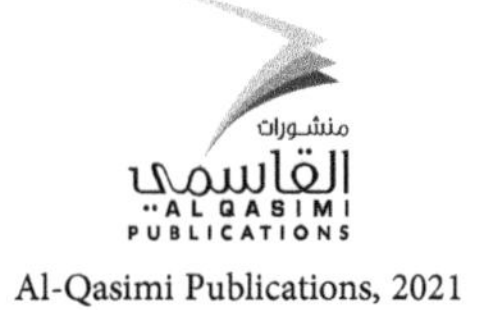

Al-Qasimi Publications, 2021

Book Title: Da'esh (ISIS) and Al Ghabra'a (Play)
First published in 2016 in Arabic as "Da'esh w Al ghabra'a" by :
Al-Qasimi Publications
Author: Dr. Sultan bin Muhammad Al-Qasimi (United Arab Emirates)
Publisher Name: Al-Qasimi Publications
Sharjah, United Arab Emirates
Edition: First
Year of publication: 2021

Translated from Arabic by: Dr. Amani Al-Sabagh

ISBN: 978-9948-469-50-6
Printing Permission: National Media Council, Abu Dhabi, UAE
No. MC 01-03-6921651, Date: 05-08-2021

Age Classification: E
The age group that matches the content of the books was classified according to the age classification issued by the National Council for Media

----

Al- Qasimi Publications, Al Tarfa, Sheikh Mohammed Bin Zayed Road
PO Box 64009 Sharjah, United Arab Emirates
Tel: 0097165090000, Fax: 0097165520070
Email: info@aqp.ae

CONTENTS

Characters

- Narrator
- A group of knights
- The Dhubyanis
- A group of Dhubyanis' Knights
- Hamal Ben Badr (Hamal son of Badr)
- His friend
- Hudayfa Ben Badr (Brother of Hamal Ben Badr)
- Followers of Hudayafa and Hamal
- A follower
- Abs Clan
- A group of the Abs's Knights
- Qays Ben Zuheir (Qays son of Zuheir)

- Malek Ben Zuheir (Brother of Quays)
- Choral
- Knight
- Call for Prayers
- Voice

Place

- Al Qaseem where you can find Ghadfan tribe with its two branches Abs and Dhubyan
- Dhubyan Clan
- Abs Clan

Time

- 50 years before the mission of Prophet Muhammed (peace be upon him)

First Scene

Narrator:

Place:

Al Qaseem where you can find Ghadfan tribe with its two branches Abs and Dhubyan

Dhubyan homes

Abs homes

Time:

50 years before the mission of Prophet Muhammed (peace be upon him).

An empty desert except for a nomadic tent, nothing can be heard except for the horses hoofs beating down the land underneath…

Two men come out of the tent, one rushes and gets ready to ride his horse (Al Ghabraa) with its dusty color and its owner is Hamal Ben Badr one of the Dhubyanis.

Far in the dark comes Quays Ben Zuheir riding his horse (Dahes) passing by Hamal Ben Badr and his friend like a lightning storm.

Hamal asks his friend saying:

Hamal Ben Badr:

"Who is that man?"

His friend:

That's Qays Ben Zuheir, one of your clans The Abs.

Hamal Ben Badr:

And what about that horse that passed by us in a blink of an eye?

His friend:

That's the matchlessly unbeatable steed-Dahes.

Meanwhile, Qays ben Zuheir riding his strutting horse returns back to the two men, then he dismounts.

Qays Ben Zuheir *(wondering)***:**

Who?... Hamal Ben Badr Al Dhubiany!!!

Hamal Ben Badr:

Good morning, cousin.

Qays Ben Zuheir:

What a lovely horse it is!!

Hamal Ben Badr:

That's Al Ghabraa... the unbeatable mare, never lost a race.

Qays Ben Zuheir:

I believe she cannot beat Dahes.

Hamal Ben Badr:

You bet?

Qays Ben Badr:

you name it.

Hamal Ben Badr:

A hundred camels go to the one who wins the race.

Qays Ben Zuheir:

I bet!

Hamal Ben Badr:

Agree?

Qays Ben Zuheir:

We've got a deal here.

The two men shake hands.

Hamal Ben Badr:

When does the race start?

Qays Ben Zuheir:

Tomorrow morning.

The two men rode their horses and kept strutting for a while showing off the slimness and beauty of their horses. Then, each headed off home.

Narrator:

Qays Ben Zuheir went to Abs homes, while Hamal Ben Badr headed to Dhubyan homes to tell their homes about the agreement.

Second Scene

Place, the end of race.

Narrator:

The race started days ago and the distance was very long, the horses had to go through desert roads and forests.

These are the vanguards of the Dhubyanis headed by Hamal Ben Badr alongside his brother Hudayfa Ben Badr and some of their fellowmen.

A fellowman:

Hamal Ben Badr! When do you expect the arrival of the two horses?

Hamal Ben Badr:

In a while.

Then he looks at his fellowmen saying:

Hamal Ben Badr:

You are going to hide in these nearby routes, if you found Dahes outrunning Al Ghabraa, distract it..

Hurry up..

Some men go away and the rest stayed with Hamal Ben Badr and Hudayfa Ben Badr.

Narrator:

Here come the vanguards of the Abs from the East led by Qays Ben Zuheir alongside his brother Malek Ben Zuheir Al Absy.

Voices *(aloud)*:

Al Ghabraa has arrived, Al Ghabraa has arrived.

Narrator:

So, Al Ghabraa has won the race.

The Dhubyanis congratulate Hamal Ben Badr on winning the race.

Meanwhile, Dahes arrives with his jockey on its back heading directly to the Abs.The jockey screams saying:

The jockey:

I was in the lead, but some people from the Dhubyanis were hiding alongside the road and they distracted the horse to let Al Ghabraa win the race. This is treason, treachery, and deceit.

Narrator:

Hudayfa Ben Badr Al Dhubyani Scolded him saying:

Hudayfa Ben Badr:

O Qays Ben Zuheir, you're the ones who are notoriously known for treachery and deceit."

Narrator:

Huzdayfa rushes barefacedly toward Qays Ben Zuheir repeatedly shouting:

Qays Ben Zuheir:

"You are the ones who are notoriously known for treachery and deceit… Known for treachery and deceit."

Qays Ben Zuheir:

"Step back, Hudayfa Ben Badr."

Narrator:

But Huzdayfa insists on challenging Qays Ben Zuheir,

(they fight)

Suddenly, Qays Ben Zheir attacks Hudayafa and kills him.

The Dhubyanis *(scream loudly)*:

"Hudayfa Ben Badr, brother of Hamal Ben Badr, is killed... Huzdayfa Ben Badr is killed."

Narrator:

"Dhubyan tribe started to attack Abs tribe, the attack resulted in killing Malek Ben Zuheir, brother of Qays Ben Zuheir.

The Abs *(scream loudly)*:

Malek Ben Zuheir (brother of Qays Ben Zuheir) is killed... Malek Ben Zuheir is killed.

Narrator:

"the Abs hold the dead body of Malek Ben Zuheir heading to their homes and so did the Dhubyanis who carried the dead body of Hudayfa Ben Badr heading to their homes.

Lamenting hums are heard

Third Scene

Narrator:

The wars have taken place for 40 years, and this is one of these wars.

A group of the Abs is marching on the East,
A group of the Dhubyanis is marching on the West.
They wear colored garments, but the linings are white, even the head covers have white linings.
And the war starts.
The rattle of the swords and the neigh of the horses are heard:
Suddenly, the Adhan (Call for prayers) is heard

The Call:

Allahu Akbar... *(God is greater).. (till the end of the call).*

While the Call was carried on …

The swords are pulled up then dropped back into dust and men rush to kneel down on their swords.

As the call for prayers was over, these men turned their garments as well as their head covers to the white side.

They abandoned their swords and headed directly to Qebla (the direction of Ka'baa in Mecca) to start praying. They hold their hands up in supplication to pray.

All men:

Allahu Akbar (God is greater) Subhan Allah (I declare the perfection of Allah from early morning to late afternoon. (till the end of the prayer).

A voice interrupting the prayer:

The Voice:

O people, Prophet Muhammed (Peace be Upon him) says:

"It is not one of us who fights fanatically for his clan,

It is not one of us who fights for his biases,

It is not one of us who dies embracing these biases."

O people, Prophet Muhammed (Peace be Upon him) says:

"O people, Allah has blessed you by purifying your souls of all the prejudices and conceit of Jahilia (pre-Islamic period). People are two kinds whether one who is pious and blessed by Allah and the other is obscene and deprived from the mercy of Allah. All people are the sons of Adam; and Adam was created of earth."

O people, Prophet Muhammed (Peace be Upon him) says:

"O People, just as you regard this month, this day, this city as Sacred, so regard the life and property of every Muslim as a sacred trust. Return the goods entrusted to you to their rightful owners. Hurt no one so that no one may hurt you. Remember that you will indeed meet your LORD, and that HE will indeed reckon your deeds. All those who listen to me shall pass on my words to others and those to others again; Did I pass it to you?

They answered:

Yes you did.

He said:

Be my witness, O Allah, that I have conveyed your message to your people, and may the last ones understand my words better than those who listen to me directly.

Never give up your faith and return to atheism killing and slaughtering each other,

Never give up your faith and return to atheism killing and slaughtering each other."

On hearing this Men get together in queues pulling up their swords saying:

All Men:

Allahu Akbar (Allah is greater, Allah is greater, Allah is greater), I bear witness that there is no God but Allah,

Allah is greater, Allah is greater. Praise be to Allah,

Allah is great. Many thanks go to Allah,

Allah, and I declare the perfection of Allah in the early morning and in the late afternoon.

I bear witness that there is no God but Allah, He fulfilled His promise, made His servant victorious, made His soldiers mighty, and defeated the allies alone.

I bear witness that there is no God but Allah, we worship no God but Him, With sincere and infinite devotion, even though the idolaters hate it.

www.ingramcontent.com/pod-product-compliance
Ingram Content Group UK Ltd.
Pitfield, Milton Keynes, MK11 3LW, UK
UKHW021959190726
13853UKWH00004B/1614